W9-AMT-220

Niki Ahrens

Lerner Publications ◆ Minneapolis

To Ms. Vivian Sink, our enchanting school librarian whose unconditional love of students and books is joyfully contagious

The photographs in this book were created by Niki Ahrens.

Lerner Publications Company
A division of Lerner Publishing Group, Inc.
241 First Avenue North
Minneapolis, MN 55401 USA

For reading levels and more information, look up this title at www.lernerbooks.com.

Main body text set in Mikado a 14/18.
Typeface provided by HVD Fonts.

Library of Congress Cataloging-in-Publication Data

Names: Ahrens, Niki, 1979– author.
Title: Moana idea lab / Niki Ahrens.
Description: Minneapolis, MN : Lerner Publications Company, [2020] | Series: Disney STEAM projects | Includes bibliographical references and index. | Audience: Age 7–11. | Audience: Grades 4 to 6.
Identifiers: LCCN 2018044203 (print) | LCCN 2018049897 (ebook) | ISBN 9781541561601 (eb pdf) | ISBN 9781541554801 (lb : alk. paper)
Subjects: LCSH: Science projects—Juvenile literature. | Handicraft—Juvenile literature. | Moana (Motion picture)—Juvenile literature.
Classification: LCC Q164 (ebook) | LCC Q164 .A355 2020 (print) | DDC 507.8—dc23

LC record available at https://lccn.loc.gov/2018044203

Manufactured in the United States of America
1-45798-42680-2/8/2019

Contents

Adventures with Moana

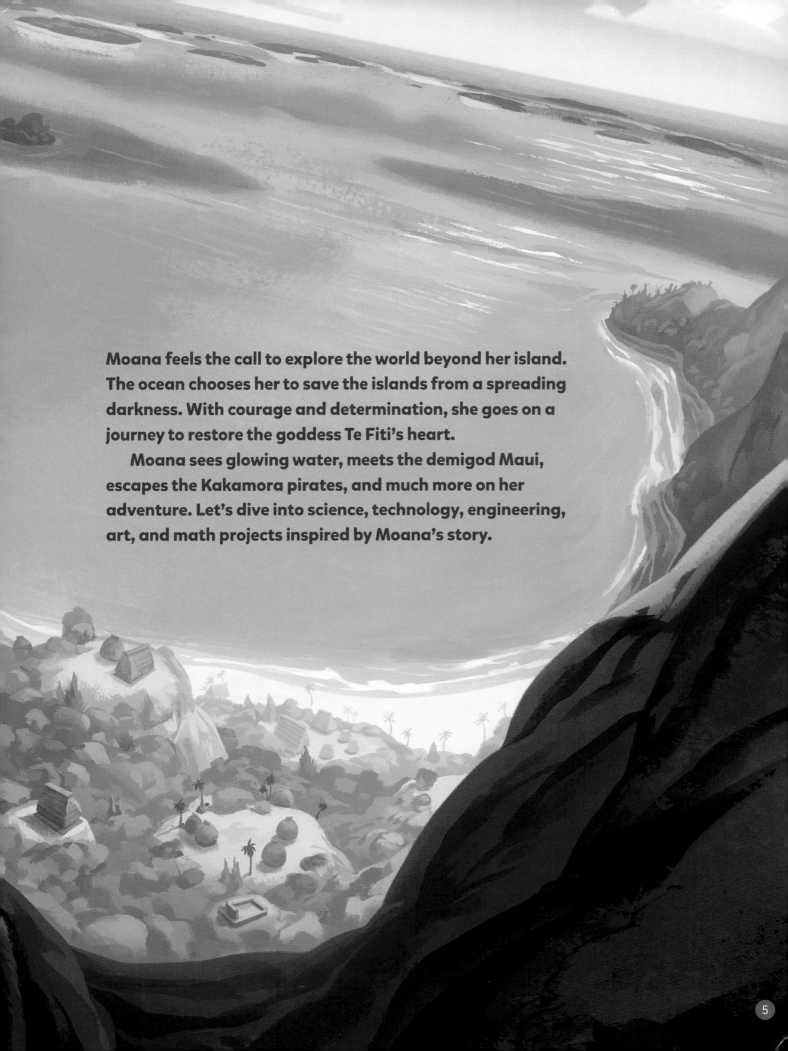

Moana feels the call to explore the world beyond her island. The ocean chooses her to save the islands from a spreading darkness. With courage and determination, she goes on a journey to restore the goddess Te Fiti's heart.

Moana sees glowing water, meets the demigod Maui, escapes the Kakamora pirates, and much more on her adventure. Let's dive into science, technology, engineering, art, and math projects inspired by Moana's story.

Before You Get Started

Each project includes a list of materials. Before you start, get what you need from home, online, or a craft or hardware store.

Choose a safe space to be your lab, and cover your workspace with newspaper. Ask an adult for permission to use sharp tools and items that might get damaged. Handle glass jars and hot water carefully. Have fun! And remember to clean up after each activity.

Glowing Water

During her adventures, Moana encounters glowing water and even living creatures that glow! You can make a jar of water glow by mixing common items.

Materials

- 2 cups (½ L) tonic water
- clear glass jar
- food coloring
- 1 tablespoon Epsom salts
- ½ teaspoon dish soap
- dark room such as a closet or bathroom
- flashlight

1. Pour the tonic water into a jar. Add two drops of food coloring.

2. Slowly pour the Epsom salts into the jar. Watch the salt make bubbles in the water.

3. Add the dish soap. Mix it in by gently swirling the jar.

4. Turn off the light, or go to a dark room. Point a flashlight at the side of the jar.

5. Watch your water glow! Use different colors to make more glowing water.

STEAM Takeaway

Bioluminescence is light that living things make with chemical reactions. Chemical reactions of the water, salt, and soap in the jar caused the water to glow. The science of how chemicals interact is chemistry.

Heart of Te Fiti Charm

The heart of Te Fiti is a bright green stone with a spiral pattern. Use homemade clay to create a charm that resembles the heart of Te Fiti.

Materials

- bowl
- 3 tablespoons cornstarch
- 1 tablespoon school glue
- 1 teaspoon vegetable or coconut oil
- spoon
- kitchen skewer
- parchment or wax paper
- watercolor paint
- paintbrush
- water
- string

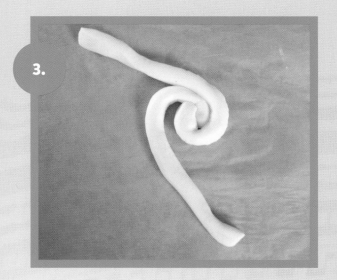

1. In a bowl, mix the cornstarch, glue, and oil together with a spoon to make clay.

2. Shape the clay into a ball with your hands. You can split the ball in half to make two charms.

3. Roll one of the balls of clay into a rope. Tear the rope in half, and shape the pieces like the swirls on the heart of Te Fiti. If the clay gets dry, add drops of oil and shape it into a ball again.

4. Gently pat the charm so it is about ¼ inch (0.6 cm) thick. Use a kitchen skewer to push a hole through your charm.

5. Set your clay on parchment or wax paper, and let it dry for 24 hours. Paint your charm, and let it dry.

6. Tie a string through your charm. You can hang it up or wear it like a necklace.

Can Hei Hei Reach a Sunken Rock?

Create a Hei Hei cork magnet, and help it reach a tasty-looking rock underwater.

Materials
- cork
- 3 hobby magnets
- 2 rubber bands
- small rock
- scissors
- clear plastic water bottle
- water

1. Wrap the cork and one magnet together with a rubber band. Wrap the rock and a second magnet together with the other rubber band.

2. Carefully use the scissors to cut off the top cone of the water bottle. Fill most of the bottle with water.

3. Place the rock magnet in the water bottle, and let it sink. Then place the Hei Hei cork magnet in the water.

4. Hold and move the third magnet along the outside of the water bottle to help the Hei Hei cork dive down to the tasty-looking sunken rock. Try to drag the sunken rock to the surface.

STEAM Takeaway

Objects float or sink in water depending on how much mass they have compared to their size. A rock tied to a magnet has a lot of mass for its size, so it sinks. A cork tied to a magnet is about the same size, but it has less mass, so it floats.

Change Its Form

Maui uses his magical hook to change forms. Use chemistry to make slime that can also shift shape.

Materials

- 4 ounces (½ cup) school glue
- sealable bowl or zip-top plastic bag
- ½ teaspoon baking soda
- 1 tablespoon water
- washable tempera paint (optional)
- spoon
- 1½ teaspoons saline solution

1. Pour the glue into the bowl or bag.

2. Add the baking soda and water. If you have tempera paint, add a small amount for color. Mix together with a spoon.

3. Slowly add the saline solution to the mixture and stir.

4. Sculpt the slime into different shapes with your hands. You can store it in a sealed container for up to 10 days.

Play a Kakamora Drumbeat

Moana and Maui meet the Kakamora pirates on their voyage. Make your own drum and play a rhythmic beat, just like the Kakamoras!

Materials

- flat-bottom coffee filter
- watercolor paint
- paintbrush
- water
- plastic jar
- rubber band
- 2 unsharpened pencils

1. Paint a coffee filter with watercolors, and allow it to dry.

2. Place and center the coffee filter over the open end of a plastic jar. Wrap a rubber band around the filter and the jar's rim to create a drum.

3. Hold two pencils so the erasers are facing up. These are your drumsticks.

4. Gently play a beat on your drum by tapping the pencils' erasers on the coffee filter.

STEAM Takeaway

Musicians hit a drum's drumhead to make sound. If the drumhead is stretched tightly on the drum, the drum makes a high sound. If the drumhead is loose, the sound is low.

Tapa Stone

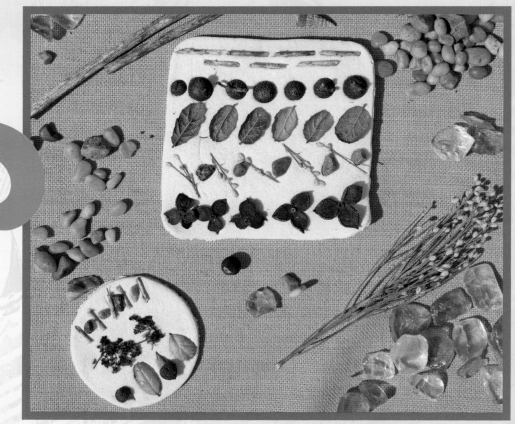

Moana's people paint the sails of their ships with designs that tell stories. Use items found in nature to tell a story on a stone.

Materials

- bowl
- ¼ cup salt
- ¼ cup water
- ½ cup flour
- spoon
- parchment paper
- rolling pin or large bottle
- small lid or drinking glass
- nature items such as pebbles, shells, seeds, and twigs

1. In a bowl, mix the salt, water, and flour with a spoon until a dough ball forms.

2. Set the dough between two sheets of parchment paper.

3. Roll the rolling pin or bottle over the parchment paper. Flatten the dough until it is about ¼ inch (0.6 cm) thick. Remove the top parchment paper.

4. Use a lid or drinking glass to cut a shape from the rolled dough. This will be your story stone.

5. Place pebbles and other found items onto the stone in a pattern to tell a story. Allow the stone to dry for 48 hours.

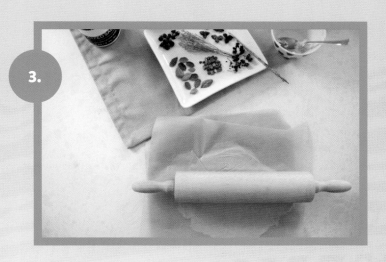

STEAM Takeaway

A tapa cloth is made from tree bark. On some Pacific islands, workers cut, soak, and then beat tree bark with a hard tool. They combine the bark to form sheets that can be decorated with designs.

Shiny Shell

Tamatoa the monster crab collects shiny things. Try making a sparkling shell like his by crystallizing an eggshell.

Materials

- egg
- small paintbrush
- school glue
- 1 plus 4 tablespoons salt
- 2 small jars
- ¼ cup measure
- hot water
- food coloring, any colors
- toothpick (optional)
- paper towel

1. Carefully crack an egg in half, and gently rinse out the two eggshell halves. Put the contents of the egg in the refrigerator for another use. Allow the eggshell to dry.

2. Gently paint the inside of each dry eggshell with glue, and sprinkle 1 tablespoon of salt inside the shells. Allow the glue to dry for 2 hours.

3. In each small jar, add ¼ cup of hot water and 3 drops of food coloring.

4. Add 2 tablespoons of salt to each jar, and stir until the salt mostly dissolves. Let the water cool to room temperature.

5.

5. Place an eggshell half into each jar until the shell is completely underwater.

6. Let the eggshells soak for 4 to 6 days. If a salt lid forms across the top of an eggshell while soaking, gently tap at the crust with a toothpick to remove it.

7. Remove the crystallized shells to dry on a paper towel. Store the shiny shells in a dry place, and watch them sparkle.

STEAM Takeaway

When salt water evaporates, the salt stays behind. The leftover salt sticks together to form sparkly crystal layers.

7.

Island in a Jar

Te Fiti can create islands and life with her heart.
You can create an island full of life in a terrarium.

Materials
- pebbles
- wide-mouth quart-size jar
- ruler
- spoon
- activated charcoal
- potting soil
- various miniature plants or seeds
- water spray bottle

1. Gently place a 1-inch (2.5 cm) layer of pebbles in the bottom of a jar.

2. Spoon a ½-inch (1.3 cm) layer of activated charcoal above the pebbles.

3. Add a 2-inch (5 cm) layer of soil on top of the charcoal.

4.

4. Place miniature plants or seeds in the soil by gently burying them near the top.

5. Spray the inside of your jar with water. Water your terrarium enough to keep the soil damp but not soaked. Check the soil each day, and water as needed.

Voyager Raft

Moana needed a good boat for her brave sea voyage to save her people and island. Build a miniature raft using sticks.

Materials

- about 10 (6-inch, or 15 cm) sticks
- scissors
- twine
- ruler
- coffee filter
- red marker
- hole punch
- 2 smaller twigs

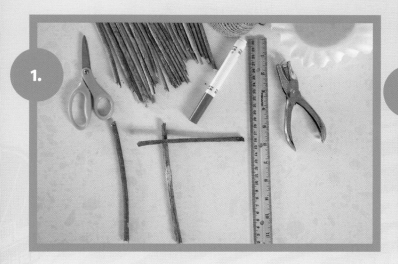

1. Choose two strong sticks to be support sticks. Place one of the support sticks underneath another stick to form a plus sign with their ends.

2. Cut two pieces of twine 6 feet (2 m) long. Use one piece to tie the top stick to the bottom support stick, leaving the stick ends in a plus sign.

3. Wrap the twine twice in each direction, forming an *X* around the sticks. Pull the twine tightly to hold the sticks in place.

4. Place the next stick beside the top one, and wrap the twine in an *X* around the new stick. Repeat with about eight more sticks. If you need more twine to secure the sticks, tie an extra piece on and continue. Tuck the twine underneath itself at the end of the row.

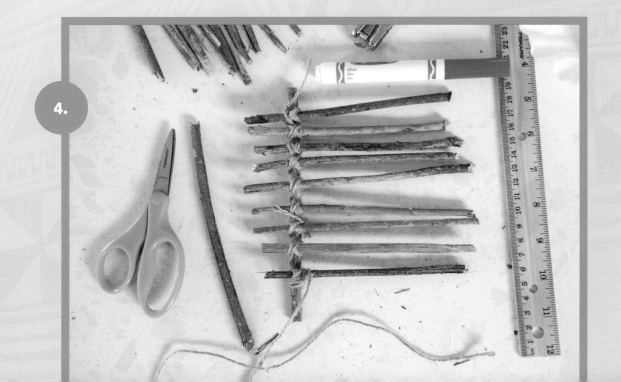

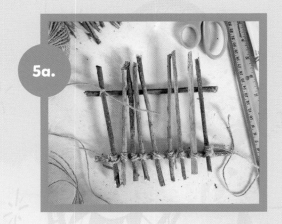

5a.

5b.

5. Place the second support stick at the other end of the raft. Thread twine between each of the sticks, and wrap them in an *X*. Tuck the twine to secure it at the end of the row.

6. Fold a coffee filter into a triangle, and decorate it with the marker.

7. Use a hole punch to make two holes along a straight side of the triangle, about 1 inch (2.5 cm) apart. Then make two holes the same distance apart on the remaining straight side of the triangle.

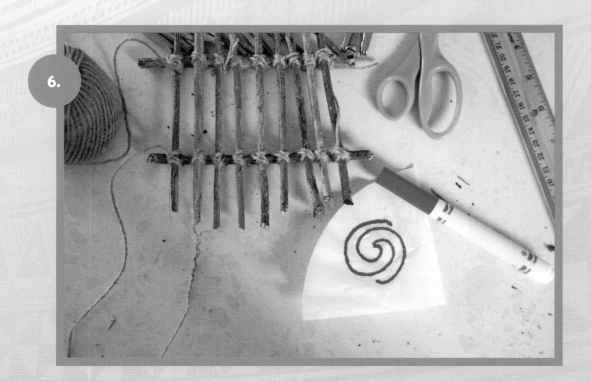

6.

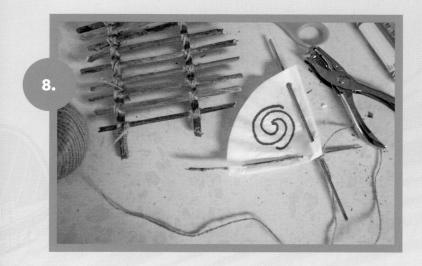

8. Slide a twig through the two holes along one side of the triangle. Do the same for the two holes on the other side of the triangle.

9. Tie twine around the two twig poles where they cross, and tie the sail to the end of the raft.

STEAM Takeaway

Moana learned to navigate at sea from Maui. He taught her about ocean weather and currents. Sea voyagers find their way by memorizing star patterns and the movement of the sun.

Glossary

bioluminescence: light that a living thing makes

charm: a decorative object often worn on necklaces or other jewelry

chemical reaction: when two or more chemicals interact to create a new substance

crystallize: to form crystals

evaporate: turn from liquid into gas

mass: an amount of matter such as metal or stone

navigate: plan a route to travel

tapa cloth: cloth from the Pacific islands made from pounded tree bark and often painted with designs or stories

terrarium: a clear container for plants or small animals

voyage: a long journey

To Learn More

Books

Dichter, Paul. *The Pacific Islands: A Moana Discovery Book*. Minneapolis: Lerner Publications, 2019.
Explore Pacific island history and culture with the cast of Disney's *Moana*.

Ives, Rob. *Fun Experiments with Matter*. Minneapolis: Hungry Tomato, 2018.
Experiment with states of matter, and learn the science behind them.

Websites

Everything You Need to Know before Seeing *Moana*
https://ohmy.disney.com/movies/2016/11/22/everything-you-need-to
-know-before-seeing-moana/
Learn more about Moana and her daring journey.

Take a Look behind the Scenes of *Moana* and 5 Years of Cultural Research
https://ohmy.disney.com/news/2016/11/07/take-a-look-behind-the
-scenes-of-moana-and-5-years-of-cultural-research/
Check out how *Moana* filmmakers learned about island cultures in the Pacific Ocean.

Index

Photo Acknowledgments

Additional image credits: Belozersky/Shutterstock.com (flask); E_K/
Shutterstock.com (gears); Aksenova Natalya/Shutterstock.com (glue),
p. 6; Olga Kovalenko/Shutterstock.com (scissors), p. 6; SJ Travel Photo
and Video/Shutterstock.com (paints), p. 7.